To the memory
of
Tessa Roger-Jones

MELISSA TO THE RESCUE

Sandy Madden

ACTES

It was a cold winter's

day.

3

Mr. Hegarty went
to see his mare.

4

"She is all right," he said.

"She is all right now."

"She is all right now but I must come back."

"She's all right now but I must come back because she is 'in foal'."

5

The next day
Mr. Hegarty went
to see his mare.

"She is **not** all right," he said.

"She is not all right now."

"She is not all right now because she has foaled and …

I can't see the foal!"

7

Mr. Hegarty
and Melissa
looked for the foal.

Melissa's brother, Connie, looked after the mare.

9

The snow was
falling a lot
and it was hard
to get along.

10

Melissa saw the foal
in the water!

11

She ran.....

and got a tyre.

She threw the tyre
over the foal's head.

She held onto the
rope.

14

Mr. Hegarty ran and got a wheelbarrow and put some straw in it.

Mr. Hegarty ran back
with the wheelbarrow
to Melissa and the foal.

16

He lifted the foal
into the wheelbarrow.

17

Up to the trailer
they ran.

They set the foal
down in front of
the fire.

The foal got warm.

It went to sleep.

Melissa went to sleep.

The next morning
Melissa saw the foal
standing up by his
mother drinking her
milk.

This all happened a few years ago around the fourteenth of February.

The foal was named Valentine.